Free to Shine

Opening The Gift of Tongues

Robert E. Colwell

Free to Shine
Opening the Gift of Tongues
Robert E. Colwell © 2015

Contact Author at: www.freetoshine.com

ISBN 978-0-9834869-9-2

Edited by:
Flo Jenkins
Words That Flo!...Editorial Consultancy Services
Torrance, CA 90501

Cover design, layout, and artwork by:
Ashley Sasson

Published by:
Latte Media Group
1030 E. Hwy 377 Suite 110 Box 184
Granbury, TX 76048

All rights reserved. No part of this book may be reproduced, scanned, or distributed in any printed or electronic form without authorized approved written permission of the author.

Neither the publisher nor the author is engaged in rendering professional advice or service to the individual reader. The ideas, suggestions, and procedures contained in this book are not intended as a substituted for consulting with your own personal professional support system.

All Scripture references are from the NKJV of the Holy Bible, unless otherwise noted.

Contents

Introduction	vii
Inner Witness	1
Clearing up Confusion	7
Why Pray in Tongues?	17
Free to Shine	29
The Unlearned	35
Intimacy	45
Give Me This Power	51
Free from Distraction (from outside)	59
Free from Distraction (from within)	65
Free from Powerlessness	71
Conclusion	81
Sources	93
About the Author	95

Introduction

Much of life is about having and handling power. Power opens the door to freedom. Personal knowledge of how it feels to be powerless is necessary in order to fully experience the power that God is pleased to impart to His people.

My earliest powerless experience occurred at age four. My tricycle bumped the wagon that my 11-month old sister was sitting in, and it rolled off the curb and emptied her behind a car that had started backing up. Too traumatized to move or speak, I sat frozen on my bike, horrified and completely powerless. My mother's panicked scream was so loud and piercing that the frightened driver pounded his brakes without looking back.

The thought of that near-disaster so burned itself into my brain that even as an adolescent I purposed to always strive to anticipate the outcome of my actions. As I grew older, I realized that a close relationship with the Lord Jesus Christ would afford the best opportunity for success at that. Reading the Bible gave me the assurance that I could always trust the Lord to help me in challenging times.

So, when my first son was born with a large opening in his back and the doctors explained to me and my wife that he may never walk or stand without the use of braces, neither have normal mental function nor the normal sense of touch, the news did not overwhelm us. Although fully aware that we were powerless in ourselves to improve his condition, peace came from knowing that God's power to handle it all was available to us through prayer.

"Peace I leave with you, My peace I give to you; not as the world gives do I give to you. Let not your heart be troubled, neither let it be afraid."

(John 14:27)

In situations wherein a person feels powerless, even strong Christians may have difficulty praying with faith and confidence (or even praying at all). This is when the Holy Spirit's grace gift of praying in tongues shows how beneficial it is; for it is that stifling

Introduction

feeling of powerlessness that this manner of praying is intended to remedy.

Of course, many believe that praying in tongues is either nonsense, of the devil, ceased with the early Church, or, at best, is a privilege reserved for chosen individuals. The following pages are intended to enlighten about the purpose and power of praying in tongues, so that all who desire to open this gift will be free to do so.

> *"You shall receive power when the Holy Spirit has come upon you; and you shall be witnesses to me in Jerusalem, and in all Judea and Samaria, and to the end of the earth."*
>
> *(Acts 1:8)*

Understandably, confusion often attends discussions about this gift. For some, to understand the truth about tongues takes little more than a fresh and close look at Scripture. Others, particularly those who have sought unsuccessfully to have this experience, may find it easier to embrace after thoughtfully considering the issue of powerlessness.

Powerlessness is, perhaps, what Mary, the sister of Lazarus, felt when she vented, *"Lord, if you had been here my brother would not have died;"* the implication was that the Lord did not care about saving His friend's life (John 11:32).

Another example of powerlessness is shown in the midst of a great storm at sea when the disciples, who were in the boat with Jesus, cried out, *"Teacher, do you not care that we are perishing?"* (Mark 4:38). This was not a logical conclusion on their part, because why would He allow them to perish when every day was spent preparing them to stand in His stead? *"How is it that you have no faith?"* was His response (Mark 4:40).

The Bible chronicles numerous statements uttered by those who felt desperate and powerless. The pressure produced by helplessness may skew our thinking and cause us to speak or react irrationally. We, therefore, may lack the power to reason in situations where we would normally apply logic. Instead, we react in a way that is senseless or absurd.

On the other hand, when the Holy Spirit infuses our prayers, He frees us from feeling powerless by bringing to our remembrance God's glorious works and attributes, and the grace poured out through the death of Jesus—God's indescribable gift (II Corinthians 9:15), (Psalms 86:8-10).

God knew that Christians in every generation would face challenges that require divine help to overcome. Therefore, the Holy Spirit was given to remind us of the truth that sets us free,

Introduction

reassuring us of God's plan for our lives, and empowering us with grace gifts to build up one another in order to deal with whatever comes our way.

The goal of this book is to help the Church experience the freedom that Christ provided through the dynamic poured out power of the Holy Spirit. It looks closely at the problem and the impact of powerlessness within the Church and embraces with urgency the task of preparing today's Christians to stand, speak, and shine undistracted. We shine whenever we display faith in the Lord and promote Christ-likeness. The devil seeks to kill our faith, steal our joy, and destroy our witness and relationships (John 10:10).

The Holy Spirit desires to help make every moment precious and victorious by freeing us from the situations, influences, and all other things that prevent us from shining.

It was the Holy Spirit who initially convinced us to surrender our lives to Jesus, and He is the Helper who guides and empowers us to do God's will every day (John 14:26).

If we lack knowledge of God's will for our lives or become distracted or powerless, it will inhibit our ability to love, hear, and view God and others as He intends. Therefore, remaining free to shine is our primary aim as Christians, and helping us to do so is the Holy Spirit's delight.

Free to Shine

Opening The Gift of Tongues

Robert E. Colwell

Praying in tongues is communing with God on a deeper, more intimate level

Inner Witness

1

To have power to witness is to be free to shine in God's kingdom here on earth. Freedom is one of life's most treasured privileges, even the freedom to speak and act in alignment with God's Word. Those who are without freedom either lacked the power to attain it, sacrificed it for what they believed to be some greater good, or temporarily relinquished it by permitting themselves to be distracted.

Remaining free to shine, therefore, is our primary aim as Christians; only then are we able to follow the Holy Spirit's leading in all things. Yet, on any given day, distractions of various sorts may prevent even the most spiritual Christian from shining—living the kingdom life—giving glory to God.

The apostle Paul endured much opposition to his efforts to advance God's kingdom ("kingdom" meaning: the sphere wherein God's rule is being carried out—where the Holy Spirit's work is obvious to those who are able to recognize it). Most of the opposition was intentional (Acts 15:36-40), though some was not (Acts 19:8-10).

Perhaps opposition aimed at ruining his image was the reason Paul, for so long, kept his Paradise experience to himself.

"I know a man in Christ who fourteen years ago – whether in the body I do not know, God knows – such a one was caught up to the third heaven. And I know such a man – whether in the body or out of the body I do not know, God knows – how he was caught up into Paradise and heard inexpressible words which it is not lawful for a man to utter."

(II Corinthians 12:2-4)

Notable is the fact that neither in the time Paul spent with the Corinthians (arriving there probably in AD 52), nor in his first letter to them (penned somewhere between AD 57-60), did Paul make any mention of the above paradise experience. After birthing that Church, teaching and demonstrating the grace gifts of the Holy Spirit, for Paul not to share with his followers this phenomenal revelation would be like a professor teaching a class on astronomy, withholding the fact that he once orbited the moon.

Paul, no doubt, was concerned that self-seeking carnal Christians might relate his experience inappropriately, using it as a weapon to make him appear foolish or irrational, thereby, thwarting his efforts to advance the gospel.

As Paul's Paradise experience was not natural, neither is the experience of praying in tongues. It affords us a powerful inner witness of our intimate personal relationship with the Lord Jesus Christ, the scope of which is not known to mere spectators.

Exercising this gift builds and renews our confidence in Christ, shapes our prayers to align more accurately with His will (I John 5:14-15), and frees us to be His witnesses by assuring us of His favor and guidance.

To witness for God is to shine. We shine whenever we display His power in any form: whether proclaiming the gospel, denying ourselves some right or pleasure for the sake of another, or apologizing for our poor actions even though others were at fault. In sum, we shine whenever our speech and actions glorify the Lord Jesus Christ who strengthens us through His Holy Spirit with power to deal with whatever comes our way (Acts 1:8;

22:14-15; John 14:26-27).

Satan wants to destroy not only our witness to God and the witness we have among others (Acts 6:3, 10:22, 22:12), but also seeks to discredit the Holy Spirit's witness to us, which is uniquely perceived through the intimacy of praying in tongues (Hebrews 2:4) (Romans 8:16).

Humankind was created to desire intimate relations with God and others. Intimacy speaks of close familiarity, that which is deep-seated and innermost. Praying in tongues is communing with God on a deeper, more intimate level. This intimacy frees us so that Christ may shine through us. Praying in tongues is a powerful reminder that God delights in the active faith expressed through the use of this gift. The realization that such prayer is authentic is sufficient in itself to inspire a greater level of faith, hope, love, and obedience to God's Word.

> *"But you shall receive power when the Holy Spirit has come upon you; and you shall be witnesses to me in Jerusalem, and in all Judea and Samaria, and to the end of the earth." (Acts 1:8)*

Inner Witness

Having power to deal with whatever comes does not mean that only positive outcomes will result from the negative situations we encounter. What it does mean is that in every situation, the confidence we gain in knowing that we have God's favor and guidance will empower us—freeing us to please our Lord every day.

People become confused when Christians treat spiritual things taught in scripture as optional

Clearing up Confusion

2

Paul's letter to the Romans is certainly one of the most important books in the Bible. Some consider it to be the most important New Testament book. Generations of Christians, particularly those who have agonized over life's ills and found no good explanation for some of the things they go through, have been encouraged by Paul's comforting words:

> *"And we know that all things work together for good to those who love God, to those who are the called according to His purpose."*
>
> *(Romans 8:28)*

Here, readers are called to trust that there is more positive activity going on with them than immediately meets the eye: God is actively involved in their life to bring about an end that is truly good—despite what they may think or feel.

Praying in tongues is somewhat similar in that it entails more than what may immediately come to mind or can be determined by reading Scripture alone. This grace gift of God must be received and opened by faith in order to fully appreciate its value. It is unequaled in its ability to:

- Deliver you into God's presence
- Heighten your sense of humility, awe, and urgency
- Remind you of your calling and relationship with the Lord
- Allow you to vent your thoughts and feelings without guilt
- Reveal that there is light at the end of your tunnel
- Reassure you that God has a purpose for your life, and that, in all things, He is working for your good

Through praying in tongues, the Holy Spirit is able to swiftly free you to stand and shine victoriously in any situation by reminding you of His nearness. Despite that truth, there are realities associated with this gift that are not dealt with directly by any one particular text, but are revealed through an abundance of Scripture and through intimate prayer over time. Statements such as "*I thank my God I speak with tongues more than you all*" (I Corinthians 14:18), may reflect Paul's understanding that one's spiritual or mental location at any given time may allow for a different experience of intimacy with God—a different urgency.

Praying in tongues is not only about the Holy Spirit speaking for you, but His witnessing to you.

The deeper the intimacy, the more open a person is likely to be in communing with God. They are likely to be more in touch with their feelings, values, and issues as well. These followers of Christ also tend to set their personal goal bar higher.

Christians who set a high bar for themselves are aware of the work involved in functioning at that higher level. Paul could, therefore, suggest to his Corinthian followers that his experience of intimacy with the Lord was deeper than theirs, and that praying in tongues inspires him to set his bar higher.

> Many Christians desire deep intimacy with the Lord, but are unlearned, distracted, or powerless to allow it to happen

Additionally, there are a number of factors that can make

praying in tongues quite confusing, even for those who regularly exercise this gift. For example, once you learn to ride a bike, you simply do it without thinking about it; likewise, a person can still speak in tongues though their mind is really somewhere else. Even falling into habitual sin may not diminish one's ability to speak in tongues.

How is this possible? It is because this power is *not derived from the act of speaking in tongues itself, but from knowledge received or activated during intimacy with God.* No intimacy, no power! General prayer is sufficient for dealing with most things most of the time; but praying in tongues is a conscious interaction with the Holy Spirit that transforms your reality and empowers you to deal with anything, anytime.

Importantly, it is not that the person who speaks in tongues is more spiritual or more connected to God than the person who does not, but that through this gift, there is instant access into the presence of the Lord; whereas for others, it may take longer to get there and require a greater stirring up of faith.

Praying in tongues while mentally disconnected from God may not produce the benefits mentioned earlier. Onlookers who observe those with un-Christian-like character speaking in tongues should assume *no fault with the gift itself or with what Scripture says* concerning it.

> "For he who speaks in a tongue does not speak to men but to God, for no one understands him; however, in the spirit he speaks mysteries"
> (1 Corinthians 14:2)

Tradition, experience, training, mental and spiritual location, etc., are some of the reasons people misapply Scripture (especially as it pertains to spiritual gifts). Yet, even if confusion were not a factor, some would continue to hold a skewed view of tongues.

Some, when hearing the words "praying in the Spirit," think exclusively of praying in tongues. However, all *genuine* prayer can be described as praying in the spirit; that is, the Holy Spirit influences what we say but does not directly assist us in saying it. This is *unassisted*, *general* prayer (praying with understanding); you simply speak the words that best convey your thoughts (I Corinthians 14:15).

Praying in tongues, on the other hand, may be better understood as praying *with* the Spirit. It is the Holy Spirit working *with* you—*assisting* you to pour out your thoughts, even those thoughts that are beyond your ability to express or understand.

It is the Holy Spirit affirming God's presence in your life, illuminating your understanding of God's attributes and promises, and freeing you to commune with God in intimacy undistracted. The power of this *intimacy* is what the devil does not want you to discover.

> *"But at midnight Paul and Silas were praying and singing hymns to God, and the prisoners were listening to them. Suddenly there was a great earthquake, so that the foundations of the prison were shaken; and immediately all the doors were opened and everyone's chains were loosed."*
>
> *(Acts 16:25-26)*

Were Paul and Silas praying and singing in tongues at that time? Scripture does not say. Surely, it is reasonable to assume that if your body had been riddled with pain after being beaten with rods and thrown into prison with your feet fastened in the stocks, you would utilize such a gift if you could.

The gospel of Luke records that on a given day as Jesus taught the people in the temple, the chief priests, scribes, and elders questioned Him as to who gave Him the authority to do the things that He did (Luke 20:1-7). He responded with a question:

Clearing-Up Confusion

"The baptism of John – was it from heaven or from men?" And they reasoned among themselves, saying, "If we say, 'From heaven,' He will say, 'Why then did you not believe Him?' But if we say, 'From men,' all the people will stone us, for they are persuaded that John was a prophet." So they answered that they did not know where it was from."

The chief priests, scribes, and elders were not free to answer Jesus truthfully because they knew the people were *persuaded* that John was a prophet. On the contrary, one of the reasons that the Church today commands so little respect is because too often our actions, both in and away from the gathered community, suggest that we are *not persuaded* in what we claim to believe.

People become confused when Christians treat the spiritual things taught in Scripture as optional. This leads them to suppose that spiritual reality turns on private interpretation.

Those who questioned Jesus wanted to know the *origin* of His authority. Most Christians today do agree that what happened on the Day of Pentecost was of divine origin; yet, many believe that, thereafter, the ability to pray in tongues was imparted to others by the hands of the original apostles only. Others hold to

Paul's teachings that praying in tongues is important for building up all Believers (I Corinthians 14:4) and should not be forbidden (I Corinthians 14:39). Still, some believe it is the doings of the misinformed.

> *Are tongues today from heaven or from men?*

If this grace gift of tongues is from heaven, then we should treat it as such. Having divine origin suggests that there may be aspects of this gift that we still may not thoroughly understand.

God's grace is poured out on everyone who turns to Him in faith. It would be inconsistent with His character to make praying in tongues available to some and not others. Paul tells us in Romans 2:11 that *"there is no partially with God."* He wants us complete, lacking nothing (James 1:4).

If God gives wisdom liberally to all who ask in faith (James 1:5), would He deny some the ability to enjoy deeper intimacy with Him, though they seek it earnestly without doubting? (James 1:6)

Some have received this gift without asking for it; although that may not be the norm, there is nothing strange about it. You should not allow anyone with limited knowledge in this area to

Clearing-Up Confusion

hinder you from seeking this experience. Often, the slightest opposition can stifle one's motivation to receive or use this gift.

Additionally, there is always the potential for abuse with certain spiritual gifts. Wisdom calls for thoughtful consideration whenever grace gifts are being operated. If confusion or deception surrounds the use of any gift, do not let that deprive you of the beautiful power that it provides. Always know that the God you serve is hearing, receiving, and responding to you with deep love.

Praying in tongues is like an injection of divine energy

Why Pray in Tongues?

3

Praying in tongues, to some, may be worthless gibberish, but to God, it is very meaningful. It is His gift to us provided for a reason. Therefore, do not allow the chorus of those who are opposed to praying in tongues keep you from embracing and enjoying this glorious gift.

Christians who reject the idea that praying in tongues is relevant today cannot conceive that any negative results could come from failing to embrace it. But what if the present fragile state of the Church is the fruit of its failure to commune with God as He intended? What if *Holy Spirit assisted prayer* is God's plan for (1) assisting His followers when their issues are overwhelming, (2) reminding them of their calling and His love for them, and (3) readying them for whatever comes their way?

Imagine how the Church would excel with confidence if Believers were reminded of these things daily through prayer. It would assure them that God is in control of their situations and prevent the kind of weakening that invites distractions and leads to powerlessness.

If praying in tongues is God's provision for building up individual Christians, then efforts to discourage such prayer amounts to giving place to the devil (Eph. 4:27). For no spiritual gift is speedier in rendering the enemy's weapons ineffective and freeing Christians to shine than Holy Spirit-assisted prayer.

> The Holy Spirit is called the Helper because God knew His followers would need his help

"But the Helper, the Holy Spirit, whom the Father will send in My name, He will teach you all things, and bring to your remembrance all things that I said to you."
(John 14:26)

Millions of people worldwide pray in tongues every day. Their hearts pour out all that they long to say, which through general prayer would take too long. Praying in tongues allows us to:

- Address issues and situations for which we have no details or facts
- Speak on things we do not yet understand
- Pray for people we do not know or whose names we do not remember
- Discuss things too difficult to put into words or that we cannot bring ourselves to speak about

General prayer is the primary way that we express and feed our understanding of the significance and trustworthiness of God's Word. It is the power supply for every good thing that a Christian will ever do. Therefore, the devil's highest priority for defeating the Christian is to discourage prayer. Knowing that nothing is more vital to our spiritual growth, he strives to convince us that general prayer is a waste of time and praying in tongues is foolish and evil.

Seizing control of the Christian's tongue remains an ambitious, demonic undertaking. For by the tongue the Lord Jesus delivered the words that forced the devil to flee from Him in the wilderness: *"Away with you, Satan! For it is written, 'You shall worship the Lord your God, and Him only you shall serve'"* (Matthew 4:1-11). Likewise, all will confess with the tongue that

Jesus Christ is Lord, to the glory of God (Philippians 2:11).

Christians grow spiritually on a diet of prayer and the study of God's Word. They build themselves up by praying in tongues, and they help build up the community of Believers by prophesying (I Corinthians 14:4). It is not strange, therefore, that much contention surrounds this issue. There is hardly a subject in the New Testament that is more passionately disputed.

In order to appreciate this gift, we must remember that *general prayer* (which is praying with understanding *only*) must be distinguished from praying in *tongues*, which is an intimate Holy Spirit-assisted conversation with the Lord. The power gained from this experience (this inner witness) is sufficient to inspire victory over anything.

The devil knows he cannot stop you from having this experience, so he deceives you into stopping yourself, and his weapon of choice is *pride*. He will bring to your attention tongues being used in a despicably inappropriate manner and then remind you that you are too intelligent and sophisticated to associate yourself with such "foolishness".

Every deception will be employed to prevent the Christian from esteeming tongues as a more intimate level of prayer. If pride does not distract you (whether your own pride or the pride of those who are jealous of your experience) then lust, suffering,

Why Pray in Tongues?

and pleasure can usually discourage this manner of praying.

For example: *lusting* for something that God clearly does not want you to have can strip away any desire you have for intimacy with God. *Suffering* can leave you too despondent to pray; and *pleasure* can make you forget, temporarily, that intimacy with God is even necessary.

> Again, praying in tongues is a grace gift of God that must be received and opened by faith

Generally speaking, *prayer* locates us and informs us of our likeness and closeness to Christ. It alerts us as to whether our eyes are fixed on the unseen promises of God, or simply on ourselves, and the things wherein we delight.

Praying in tongues goes further in that it assures us that our prayers have been heard and understood; for we are confident that the sounds coming out of our mouth did not originate with us, but the Holy Spirit Himself speaks through us (Romans 8:27).

And despite ample personal and scriptural evidence of the relevance of tongues, many have abandoned without reservation what Paul took nearly an entire chapter to set in order (1 Corinthians 14). "*He who speaks in a tongue edifies himself*"

(I Cor. 14:4). *"I wish you all spoke with tongues"* (I Corinthians 14:5). *"I thank my God I speak with tongues more than you all"* (I Cor. 14:18).

Paul, in his letter to the Galatians, admonishes the Christian community of Believers not to allow those who are ignorant of the finished work of Christ to influence what they believe.

"I marvel that you are turning away so soon from Him who called you in the grace of Christ, to a different gospel...."

(Galatians 1:6)

History has shown that beliefs, along with the words that shape them, may change, weaken, or become lost over time if not nurtured. A good example of this is seen in how quickly Israel's knowledge of God dwindled into insignificance after the death of Joshua and the elders after Joshua, who reminded Israel of the great works of God.

"So the people served the Lord all the day of Joshua, and all the days of the elders who outlived Joshua, who had seen all the great works of the Lord which He had done

for Israel."

(Judges 2:7)

"When all that generation had been gathered to their fathers, another generation arose after them who did not know the Lord nor the work which He had done for Israel. Then the children of Israel did evil in the sight of the Lord and served the Baals; and they forsook the Lord God of their fathers, who had brought them out of the land of Egypt; and they followed other gods from among the gods of the people who were all around them, and they bowed down to them; and they provoked the Lord to anger."

(Judges 2:10-12)

Scholars differ on whether the word "know" in the above statement (did not *know* the Lord) refers to ignorance or failure to acknowledge God. The context seems to suggest deficiency in knowledge—lacking awareness, *being unlearned*. Regardless of which is correct, the outcome was the same; they did evil in the sight of the Lord, displaying behavior typical of people who know little or nothing of God or His ways.

When God's Word is truly heard, it reshapes our entire outlook on life. We are then moved by our perception of what it means to belong to God, to afford Him proper respect and adoration. We respond to His Word as if He is visibly present with us. Solomon wrote: *"Where there is no revelation, the people cast off restraint"* (Proverbs 29:18). The King James Version reads: *"Where there is no vision, the people perish."*

What it means is that if there is nothing and no one to remind people of what God has said or done, the people will cease doing what is right—that which God has instructed them to do.

Examples of this are everywhere. For instance, a concerned mother recently asked me to talk with her 20-year-old son who had come home on spring break from a reputable Christian University. She noticed his attitude toward God had become disturbingly casual and that he now prays only if asked, which was uncharacteristic of him.

When I arrived at their home, John was watching a movie but was willing to stop and talk with me. After opening our discussion with prayer, I asked about his personal prayer life, which he acknowledged had been somewhat inconsistent.

After explaining to him the significance of prayer and its importance in my life, I asked if he had ever experienced praying in tongues. He sat back in his chair and then answered me with the question that his professor had recently proposed to his class:

Why Pray in Tongues?

"Is there any significance in praying in tongues today?"

Before answering, I thought it best to hear how his classmates responded. He explained that the one student who answered yes was stiffly opposed by the professor, who then qualified his response by stating that his position aligns with that of the school.

Unfortunately, this scenario is played out increasingly in today's high school and college classrooms where Christians are identified as "bad guys", and the teacher becomes the self-appointed sheriff who then deputizes the other students to assist in making the arrest. This victimization of Christians has become a popular politically-correct amusement that has its supporters salivating at the prospects of winning government sanctions for all their ideologies.

"So why did you not speak up in support of the brave student?" I asked. "You grew up hearing your mother pray in tongues, didn't you?" "Yes," he replied, "but I'm not exactly sure what I believe. No one ever talks about tongues anymore, and had the professor not raised the issue, it would never have come up." He went on to question the relevance of tongues by citing a recent family heartbreak that praying in tongues did not prevent.

Herein is the reason that the Church (particularly here in the

West) is experiencing such rapid decline in true spirituality. For where there is no reminder (no Joshua)—no witnesses to declare the ways of God, the spirituality of the people will perish and they will cease doing what is right.

Consider that not long ago non-Christians were obliged to show respect for the Church, as long as they were not inconvenienced by Christian practices. There was a moral limit line that they made an effort not to cross; yet today, most non-Christians view the message and conduct of conscientious Christians as a nuisance that needs to go away. A contributing factor is the willingness of self-absorbed Christians to embrace worldly trends that are inconsistent with what they know to be the will of God.

Furthermore, "success" has turned many churches into breeding grounds for selfishness, bigotry, and carnality. Their young people appear to be on fire for Jesus and the older folks contribute their time, energy, and finances faithfully. Deficient levels of spirituality are not detected until disappointment or affliction arises, as with illness or loss.

Christians who shun praying in tongues overlook (or are simply ignorant of) the fact that this power-gift comes from God and is perfect for accomplishing what He intends. *"Every good and every perfect gift is from above and comes down from the Father of lights"* (James 1:17).

Why Pray in Tongues?

Praying in tongues is like an injection of divine energy. The Holy Spirit not only speaks *for* you, but also witnesses *to* you, assuring you of His presence. Its ability to inspire, build faith, and give hope can be as powerful as experiencing an indisputable miracle. This level of relationship with God is transforming and profound; therefore, consider the enormity of Satan's victory in deceiving generations of Christians to resist praying in tongues. Imagine the difference in a person's personal relationship with God, in evangelism, and fellowship with other Christians if even a small percentage of Christians in each Church prayed in tongues.

The Church community, without question, has been severely impacted by society's moral implosion. God promised that with every temptation, He would make a way of escape that His followers would be able to bear it (I Corinthians 10:13). The gift of praying in tongues is a means of escape that the Church would do well to embrace...*now*.

Despite diminished levels of spirituality, particularly among young people, many Christian leaders avoid teaching about praying in tongues or apply little significance to it. Leaders who do not routinely use this gift should encourage and build excitement among their followers to further explore it together.

Failure to shine in any area is the result of not being free to do so. Something is in the way...

Free to Shine

4

We all enjoy having people view us favorably. Few things in life are more gratifying than shining victoriously in the presence of others. And whether through competition, challenge, knowledge, wisdom, or good character, precious are those moments wherein through God's grace, we shine.

> *"You are the light of the world," Jesus exhorted His followers; "A city that is set on a hill cannot be hidden. Nor do they light a lamp and put it under a basket, but on a lamp stand, and it gives light to all who are in the house. Let your light so shine before men, that they may see*

Free to Shine

your good works and glorify your Father in heaven"
(Matthew 5:14-16)

To shine is to be a witness for the Lord. Shining occurs as we demonstrate unashamedly an awareness of God's active presence in our lives, a presence marked by love, faith, and hope. We shine whenever these three unite on any issue or in any situation wherein we remain unmoved by society's ills and life's distractions.

Failure to shine in any area is the result of not being free to do so. Something is in the way—hindering, distracting, or rendering us powerless. And regardless of how we personally view ourselves, our actions place us into one of four categories:

- Unlearned
- Distracted
- Powerless
- Free to Shine

> *Freedom allows us to act in faith; powerlessness hinders our ability to act at all*

No one, of course, was ever freer than our Lord Jesus Christ,

Free to Shine

Who even in the face of death was free to respond appropriately to friend and foe alike.

> *"Then Pilate said to Him, 'Are you not speaking to me? Do you not know that I have power to crucify you, and power to release you?' Jesus answered, 'You could have no power at all against me unless it had been given you from above'"*
>
> *(John 19:10-11)*

No doubt Pilate was surprised by Jesus' answer, but, perhaps even more so with His tone.

> *"Pilate therefore said to Him, 'Are You a king then?' Jesus answered, 'You say rightly that I am a king. For this cause I was born, and for this cause I have come into the world, that I should bear witness to the truth. Everyone who is of the truth hears My voice.' Pilate said to Him, "What is truth?"*
>
> *(John 18:37-38)*

So impacting was that truthful tone in Jesus' voice that despite the accusations hurled against Him and cries of the crowds,

Pilate was moved to declare: *"I find no fault in Him at all"* (John 18:38).

Truth has a certain tone—an intonation that expresses resolve—indicating the speaker's sureness of mind. It gives evidence of God's influence and is typically delivered assertively, marked by confidence. Nothing generates a more resounding truthful tone than intimate communion with God.

In Acts 19:13-16, we see that the sons of Sceva attempted to address a spiritual situation without the help of the Helper (God's Spirit). Claiming to have authority that they did not have, they offended the evil spirit by issuing a command with no truthful tone in their voice (no Helper) to back it up.

"Then some of the itinerant Jewish exorcists took it upon themselves to call the name of the Lord Jesus over those who had evil spirits, saying, 'We exorcise you by the Jesus whom Paul preaches.' Also there were seven sons of Sceva, a Jewish chief priest, who did so. And the evil spirit answered and said, 'Jesus I know, and Paul I know; but who are you?' Then the man in whom the evil spirit was leaped on them, overpowered them, and prevailed against them, so that they fled out of that house naked and wounded."

In this situation, mere knowledge of power was not enough. These were sons of the chief priest, raised in the disciplines of God's Law. However, at some point after seeing Paul's miracles, they tried to mimic his actions but quickly learned they could not. Their lack of authority resounded in their tone.

Likewise today, many desiring to have this power may mimic praying in tongues and fool some, but more often than not, their tone will betray them. This tone (not the audible sound of one's voice, but a tone of truth and confidence) is developed through prayer and obedience to God's Word, but is further developed through the soul-freeing experience of Spirit-assisted prayer. It is available to every Christian who seeks it unwaveringly.

> *"Now this is the confidence that we have in Him, that if we ask anything according to His will, He hears us. And if we know that he hears us, whatever we ask, we know that we have the petitions that we have asked of Him"*
> *(I John 5:14-15)*

Later, we will discuss this further.

The gift of praying in tongues is given to those who see it as a personal necessity and pursue it in faith with an eye toward advancing God's kingdom here on earth

The Unlearned

5

The New Testament uses the term "babes" to describe Christians who have not yet learned about the things of God (Romans 2:20; I Corinthians 3:1). We find in Acts 8:9-24 the story of an apparent babe named Simon.

> *9) But there was a certain man called Simon, who previously practiced sorcery in the city and astonished the people of Samaria, claiming that he was someone great, 10) to whom they all gave heed, from the least to the greatest, saying, 'This man is the great power of God.' 11) And they heeded him because he had astonished them with his sorceries for a long time. 12) But when they believed Philip as he preached the things concerning the kingdom of God and the name of Jesus Christ, both men and women were baptized. 13) Then Simon*

himself also believed; and when he was baptized he continued with Philip, and was amazed, seeing the miracles and signs which were done.

14) Now when the apostles who were at Jerusalem heard that Samaria had received the word of God, they sent Peter and John to them, 15) who when they had come down, prayed for them that they might receive the Holy Spirit. 16) For as yet He had fallen upon none of them. They had only been baptized in the name of the Lord Jesus. 17) Then they laid hands on them, and they received the Holy Spirit.

18) And when Simon saw that through the laying on of the apostles' hands the Holy Spirit was given, he offered them money, 19) saying, "Give me this power also, that anyone on whom I lay hands may receive the Holy Spirit."

20) But Peter said to him, 'Your money perish with you, be cause you thought that the gift of God could be purchased with money! 21) You have neither part nor portion in this matter, for your heart is not right in the sight of God. 22) Repent therefore of this your wickedness, and pray God if perhaps the thought of your heart may be forgiven you. 23) For I see that you are poisoned by

The Unlearned

bitterness and bound by iniquity.'

24) Then Simon answered and said, 'Pray to the Lord for me, that none of the things which you have spoken may come upon me'"

(Acts 8:9-24).

As stated in the previous chapter, we all enjoy being viewed favorably. Simon no doubt enjoyed being esteemed as the *great power of God* and likely profited well from his sorcery. Accustomed to the praise of men and knowing well the fraud of sorcery, he was amazed at the genuine miracles and signs done by Philip.

Upon hearing Philip's preaching of the gospel and seeing the response of the people to the miracles, Simon also believed and was baptized. Yet something was in his way not allowing his heart to be pure before God; he was obsessed with having the power that resulted from the *"laying on of the apostles' hands"* (Acts 8:18).

The fact that this power came from God may have mattered little to Simon; he would have made the purchase regardless of its source. He was struck by the prospect of being able to bestow upon others an enraptured state for which they would praise him and pay handsomely.

Free to Shine

Christian life should be marked by a commitment to truth; yet, you can always find people in the Church who are content with being a fake. This is often because they are pursuing some selfish agenda, covering up for some failure, or are unlearned—lacking sufficient knowledge of the Savior Jesus Christ. They often display behavior similar to that of un-Believers. Rather than despise them, we must keep in mind that they may be "babes" (as we once were) and may likely be wrestling with a number of issues.

It would be hasty to assume from Simon's selfish request for power that he had not truly surrendered his life to the Lord. Scripture says that he believed (Acts 8:13). The early Church did not baptize people in hopes that they would eventually accept Christ, rather, only when it was reasonable to believe they *already had*.

Everyone who accepts Jesus Christ as their Lord and Savior receives both forgiveness of sins and the indwelling Holy Spirit at the point of conversion. The power that Simon saw being demonstrated at the hands of the apostles was the opening of the gift of the Holy Spirit -- God's grace gift in operation, readying individuals to accept the *ongoing work* of the *Holy Spirit*, helping them and reaching through them to help and minister to others (Acts 8:18).

The Unlearned

This grace gift of tongues does not open automatically with conversion and water baptism, nor is it initially poured out on those who seek it with wrong motives.

"You ask and do not receive because you ask amiss, that you may spend it on your pleasures."

(James 4:3)

Before the gift of tongues will open for anyone, the Holy Spirit must cleanse their heart so that God alone gets the glory (glory which Simon surely would have claimed for himself). Simon could have mimicked (faked) speaking in tongues, but could do nothing, of himself, to make it happen.

This gift of praying in tongues opens for those who see it as a personal necessity and pursue it in faith with an eye toward advancing God's kingdom here on earth.

> *Praying in tongues is not natural;*
> *it is a spiritual experience*

We see in Acts 15:23-24 that the apostles and elders wrote a letter to the Gentile brethren who were being discouraged by Christian leaders who did not want to abandon the Jewish tradition of circumcision. They had not learned to trust in the finished work of Christ:

"Since we have heard that some who went out from us have troubled you with words, unsettling your souls saying, 'You must be circumcised and keep the law' – to whom we gave no such commandment –...."

(Acts 15:23-24)

Similarly, there are Church leaders today who, with good intentions but without commandment from the Lord, have discouraged followers from embracing the gift of tongues. The current opposition to the spread of the gospel is so great that it is imperative that the body of Christ be thoroughly equipped with every provision for the work of the ministry (Ephesians 4:12).

Evidence of the need for revival (spiritual renewal) is everywhere; yet, the grace gift that is able to spark renewal is taught by some to be no longer in operation. They believe that *speaking in tongues* occurred only in the first century and solely for getting the gospel out to people of other languages (Acts 2:4-8). They believe that what the Samaritans experienced in Acts 8:14-17 is identical to what occurred on the day of Pentecost.

The Unlearned

"And they were all filled with the Holy Spirit and began to speak with other tongues, as the Spirit gave them utterance. And there were dwelling in Jerusalem Jews, devout men, from every nation under heaven. And when this sound occurred, the multitude came together, and was confused, because everyone heard them speak in his own language. Then they were all amazed and marveled, saying to one another, 'Look, are not all these who speak Galileans? And how is it that we hear, each in our own language in which we were born?'"

(Acts 2:4-8)

"Now when the apostles who were at Jerusalem heard that Samaria had received the word of God, they sent Peter and John to them, who when they had come down, prayed for them that they might receive the Holy Spirit. For as yet He had fallen upon none of them. They had only been baptized in the name of the Lord Jesus. Then they laid hands on them, and they received the Holy Spirit."

(Acts 8:14-17)

Nothing in the Acts 8:14-17 account suggests that anyone in the Samaritan's house heard their own language spoken by those who were praying in tongues. Peter and John's purpose for traveling to Samaria was to provide clarity and assistance to recent converts. Clarity is needed even today to understand the empowerment that takes place at conversion.

When conversion takes place, the Believer is justified before God and inherits God's *future* kingdom; but the *present* kingdom (God's rule displayed in the Christian's life here on earth) is experienced only through faith-filled-obedience to God's Word. This present Kingdom is realized by those who believe that its treasure (righteousness, joy in the Holy Spirit, peace, love, power, etc.) is of great value.

> *Do we receive all available power at the point of conversion?*

Imagine, for example, you inherited a house that had a wall safe that you could not open. Not having access to its treasure would not prevent you from enjoying life, but opening the safe might allow you to live life on another level.

And so it is with the gift of praying in tongues. This gift opens

The Unlearned

for those who believe that inside is a treasure of great value—a deeper intimacy with the all-knowing, all-powerful God.

The Holy Spirit was *with* us prior to our conversion. He came alongside us to convince us to surrender our lives to the Lord. Once we opened our heart, He then came *in* us, giving us power to say yes to God's will and to resist all that is not compatible with His way. Then in response to our soul's longing for intimacy with God, the Holy Spirit came *upon* us, empowering us to deny ourselves and to reach out to others that they may also learn of Him.

Simon obviously had not yet learned to *"deny himself"* (Matthew 6:33) or to *"set his mind on things above and not on things on the earth"* (Colossians 3:2). What then should we conclude concerning him? It is easy to disapprove of a person who has made a mistake or is unlearned; but finding reasons to approve of such a one may call for the Holy Spirit's help.

How marvelous to serve a God Who has made a way to approve of sinners and for them to be intimate with Him in prayer. Perhaps once we enter God's future kingdom, we will know not only if Simon ever opened this gift of the Spirit, but also of the many others who prevailed through the use of it.

The gift of tongues opens in intimacy

Intimacy

6

Those who truly become born again find pleasure in the truth and begin to judge all things by God's standard of love and righteousness. Yet alarmingly, many churches have buckled beneath today's anti-Christian influence and now find other standards to be suitable, such as: "appearance" (that which looks good to the eye), political correctness (that which sits well with the dominant culture), and happiness, etc.

Judging by different standards is probably the root of most strained relationships, particularly in marital unrest. The standard of judgment for Christians must be Christ's love and righteousness as revealed in His Word. In Amos 3:3, the prophet asks: *"Can two walk together, unless they are agreed?"*

A standard is something used as a *rule* or basis for comparison in measuring or judging capacity, quantity, content, extent, value, quality, etc.[1] We are admonished in Philippians 3:16 to *"Walk by the same rule... be of the same mind."*

Every rule begins with a vision. For example, most of us have a vision of how we would like our home to run. Requiring others to align with our vision is an attempt to establish it as a rule. As others decide to apply this same rule to their homes, it may then become a standard.

Problems arise when one spouse thinks and acts according to the standard of Christ's love and righteousness while the other makes decisions based on need or happiness, etc., and then applies that standard to decisions even about the marriage itself.

Maintaining close relationships is difficult enough when each party measures by the same rule; but trying to enjoy closeness with a person whose standard of judgment is different strains the relationship, forcing one party—if not both—to compromise their convictions.

God's vision for relationships is intimacy, whether between God and humankind, or among members of the Believing community. God intends for His followers to love, serve, and depend on one another, not to simply be satisfied with glancing nods

Intimacy

and handshakes after the Sunday morning service.

Intimacy is what God enjoyed with Adam in the Garden of Eden prior to their relationship being tainted by sin. The process to restore intimacy entailed God dwelling with humankind in the person of Jesus Christ (Matthew 1:23), who humbled Himself in obedience, even to the death of the Cross (Philippians 2:8).

If we, in turn, humble ourselves and draw near to Him, He will draw near to us (James 4:8). But how near is near? To one person, "near" is within earshot; to another, it is being able to almost touch. The Psalmist's desire to be close to the Lord prompted him to write:

"My soul longs, yes, even faints for the courts of the Lord."

(Psalms 84:2)

Intimacy with God is what our soul really longs for. On a natural level, the word *intimacy* (like the English word *love*) has been stretched to fit an array of human situations. The word *natural* refers to what is common or usual, as distinguished from the *spiritual*. More importantly, however, on a spiritual level, the intimacy that the human soul longs for is possible only through a relationship with Jesus Christ.

Our God seeks intimacy (individually and corporately) with His followers. This intimacy is what sets Christianity apart from all religions. It produces keen awareness that our sufficiency is in God (II Corinthians 3:5) and through Christ we can do all that He places on our heart to do (Philippians 4:13).

A significant factor in true intimacy is that each party must believe that mutual attention is being devoted to the weightiest of matters with a similar degree of urgency. Therefore, intimacy is all about gaining and sharing knowledge that is unique to a treasured time and space.

Whenever motivation for intimacy fades, selfishness and individualism abound. Unfortunately, these two relationship busters are heavily promoted and celebrated in today's society. They feed much confusion—particularly among the younger generation, which is often ill-equipped to fend against the world's lure of pleasure and popularity.

And how should we respond to these enemies of intimacy? Is there no remedy? Is our only defense to outrun the enemy by finding creative new ways to make Church fun for the young-hearted? Is intimacy with God reserved for super-spiritual adults, or is it a practice intended to shape the believing community?

Praying in tongues is engaging God in intimacy with a greater degree of urgency. Like pushing a personal reset button, it frees us to gain a fresh perspective on what it means to be the people of God.

Self-seeking Christians were undoubtedly as much of a problem for the early church as they are today

Give Me This Power

7

What if Simon had not offered money to buy the divine power from the apostles but kept that thought within? Would he have spoken in tongues along with the other disciples when the apostles laid hands on them? There are a number of reasons to believe the answer is no. Simon's heart was not right before God (Acts 8:21), he was driven by wrong motives, harbored bitterness in his heart, was bound by iniquity (Acts 8:23), and showed no interest in advancing his relationship with the Lord.

We all have entertained desires or pursued issues that were contrary to God's Word and succumbed to distractions that resulted in adverse circumstances. Yet, we still came away with the testimony: "*that all things work together for good to those who love God, to those who are the called according to His purpose*" (Romans 8:28).

Other than unbelief, *distraction* is the greatest inhibitor to speaking in tongues. The mind must be free to focus on the majesty of the Lord; otherwise, it is unlikely that the gift of tongues will open. Simon was no doubt distracted by the power he saw operating in the evangelist Philip and was filled with excitement over the idea of advancing his own fame among the people (Acts 8:19).

Those desiring to pray in tongues must resolve that God does not respect one person above another (Romans 2:11). He intends for all His gifts to be used for the benefit of the community of Believers. Yet, for many Christians, as with Simon, there may be certain factors that get in the way, many times unknowingly. Those seeking to have this experience should begin by casting down any lust for power or fame.

"...Casting down arguments and every high thing that exalts itself against the knowledge of God, and bringing every thought into captivity to the obedience of Christ."
(II Corinthians 10:5)

Lust for fame is a mindset that is incompatible with Christ

and a hindrance to praying in tongues. Again, your thoughts should be centered on the Lord. Fame is the engine of secular value systems. Webster's Dictionary defines fame as: *the state of being well known or much talked about; celebrity.*[2] It should never drive the Church.

Fame benefits private individuals and affords significant personal advantage for them. It plays to a different standard and clashes with the aim of Scripture, which is to equip Christians to serve and shine within the body of Christ and be salt and light to the world (Phillipians 2:15).

The word "*serve*" speaks of meeting the needs of others; it is the rendering of any kind of service. This same Greek word (diakoneo) also means *ministering*, which is one of the grace gifts mentioned in Romans chapter twelve.

> *"Having then gifts differing according to the grace that is given to us, let us use them: if prophecy, let us prophesy in proportion to our faith; or ministry, let us use it in our ministering..."*
>
> *(Romans 12:6-7)*

Self-seeking Christians were undoubtedly as much of a problem for the early church as they are today.

"But I trust the Lord Jesus to send Timothy to you shortly, that I also may be encouraged when I know your state. For I have no one like-minded who will sincerely care for your state. For all seek their own, not the things which are of Christ Jesus. But you know his proven character, that as a son with his father he served with me in the gospel."

(Philippians 2:19-21)

If fame happens while pursuing goals that do not violate Kingdom life, then so be it—all glory to God; but to make fame the goal is to immerse oneself into a secular value system that always clashes with the way of the Christ. As Christians, we are to turn from any *fame-driven* system to the *servant-driven* values to which we were called (Galatians 5:13).

Christians are to be other-directed—seeking first the kingdom of God and trusting in His care and provision. Simon, no doubt, was thinking of his personal advancement when asked to purchase the divine gift (Acts 8:18-19). The book of James reveals: "*If you abide in Me, and My words abide in you, you will ask what you desire, and it shall be done for you*" (John 15:7).

The Lord delights to see His followers shine to the glory of God, always ready to deal with the trials ahead. The present moral decline in society and rising animosity against the Christian community makes the need to shine an urgency.

"But even if you should suffer for righteousness' sake, you are blessed. And do not be afraid of their threats nor be troubled. But sanctify the Lord God in your hearts, and always be ready to give a defense to everyone who asks you a reason for the hope that is in you, with meekness and fear..."

(I Peter 3:14-15)

The anti-God community is celebrating what they perceive to be a victory. The Church appears unable to escape the power of their immoral pursuits. Disturbing are the statistics on young people falling away from the faith; even mentioning it feels like giving glory to the devil.

Scripture informs us that "*All who desire to live godly in Christ will suffer persecution*" and that "*evil men and impostors will grow worse and worse*" (II Timothy 3:12). Yet Isaiah 59:19 reminds us that, "*When the enemy comes in like a flood, The Spirit of the lord will lift up a standard against him.*"

Prayer is a remedy for powerlessness and aggression against the Church.

Many acknowledge the need for greater spirituality within the Church and a closer personal connection with God. Praying in tongues moves us closer towards that goal. It affords us a revitalizing Spirit-assisted conversation with the Lord that helps to provide a right perspective on every situation that a Christian encounters. It is a divine prescription for anxiety and complacency.

Many Christians confess their openness to receive this gift but believe that no action on their part is necessary to acquire it. "If God wants me to have it," they say, "*then He knows how to give it to me.*"

Undistracted Christians who recognize their need for deliverance, do not sit around hoping to one day attract the Lord's attention to their issue.

- Matthew 7:7 "*Ask, and it will be given to you; seek and you will find; knock, and it will be opened to you.*"
- Psalms 34:14 "*...seek peace and pursue it;*"
- Psalms 105:4 "*Seek the Lord and His strength; seek His face evermore!*"
- James 1:22 "*But be doers of the word, and not hearers only, deceiving yourselves.*"

Some things, as is often the case with opening the gift of

Give Me This Power

tongues, call for more than just a casual interest. In John 12:20-37, certain Greeks who had come to worship at the feast said to Philip, *"Sir, we wish to see Jesus."* The Greek word (zeloo) means earnestly desire—to be positively and intensely interested in something.[3]

Having more than just a casual interest is what Paul, no doubt, encouraged among his followers, and is perhaps why he wraps up his teaching on spiritual gifts with these instructions: *"But earnestly desire the best gifts. And yet I show you a more excellent way"* (I Corinthians 12:39).

John's Epistle records:

"That if we ask anything according to His will, He hears us. And if we know that He hears us, whatever we ask, we know that we have the petitions that we have asked of Him."

(I John 5:14-15)

Distraction is the enemy of every endeavor

Free from Distraction (from outside)

8

Imagine the terror of an approaching enemy as numerous as locusts on a field. This is what the 32,000 men of Israel who responded to Gideon's call to battle faced. The massive combined army of Midianites and Amalekites were encamped in the valley beneath where the Israelites were located.

The enemy's "*...camels were without number, as the sand by the seashore in multitude*" (Judges 7:12).

Although the Midianites were descendants of Abraham through his son Midian by his later wife Keturah, they were never considered to be a part of the covenant people. Most likely they were aware of Israel's history and the miraculous victories won for them, but their actions proved their ignorance regarding God's favor and commitment to Israel.

Yet, despite all that God's mighty hand accomplished for Israel in the past, the size of the Midianite and Amalekite armies presented a major distraction for them. So, the Lord instructed Gideon to have all who were fearful and afraid to return to their homes; 22,000 without hesitation went back. Gideon was left with just 10,000 men who were willing to trust God.

One of the things we learn from this story is that not everyone who is *willing* to trust God is actually *free* to do so. This is largely the reason the Lord informed Gideon that the 10,000 remaining men were still too many for Him to grant them a victory; for they would glorify themselves, claiming that their own mighty hand won the battle (Judges 7:2). God then further reduced their number by 9,700, using only the 300 that were free to follow Him undistracted.

> *Just as truth has a certain tone, freedom has a certain appearance*

4) But the Lord said to Gideon, "The people are still too many; bring them down to the water, and I will test them for you there. Then it will be, that of whom I say to you,

Free From Distraction (from outside)

'This one shall go with you,' the same shall go with you; and of whomever I say to you, 'This one shall not go with you,' the same shall not go." 5) So he brought the people down to the water. And the Lord said to Gideon, "Everyone who laps from the water with his tongue, as a dog laps, you shall set apart by himself; likewise everyone who gets down on his knees to drink." 6) And the number of those who lapped, putting their hand to their mouth, was three hundred men; but all the rest of the people got down on their knees to drink water. 7) Then the Lord said to Gideon, "By the three hundred men who lapped I will save you, and deliver the Midianites into your hand. Let all the other people go, every man to his place."

(Judges 7:4-7)

No doubt there was great excitement throughout the camp initially in seeing the 22,000 return without a scratch. But the jubilation was short-lived when they learned that the other 10,000 were left to fight alone. Perhaps, while these 22,000 were still trying to explain why they returned, another 9,700 showed up armed with the face-saving excuse that they were ordered to go home by Gideon.

Free to Shine

Whether faced with shameful embarrassment or debilitating fear, we shine only as we are *free* to trust God and confront our issues undistracted.

The Angel of the Lord could refer to Gideon as a "mighty man of valor" (Judges 6:12) not because of Gideon's courage, but because knowing that God was with him was all that he needed in order to shine (Judges 6:1). This same sense of God's presence is available to us in Spirit-assisted prayer.

Imagine the suffering throughout the Israelite camp in thinking about the fate of the 300, and then the exhilarating victory celebration when the 300 returned!

What a powerful lesson about trusting God and not allowing what we see to distract us.

> *How often we fret over situations that the Lord already resolved*

Free From Distraction (from outside)

Knowing that God was with him was all that he needed in order to shine.

Distractions pave the way for powerlessness

Free from Distraction (from within)

9

Knowing all too well the emotions, feelings, and thoughts that can accompany the birth of a child that has a serious disability, the miracle of Jesus opening the eyes of the man born blind was particularly "eye-opening" for me. Our first son was born with a serious spinal cord defect. We were told that he might not walk or stand without braces, or have normal mental function or the normal sense of touch. Therefore, it is easy for me to imagine what the parents in this story must have endured (John 9). Never had they prayed more earnestly for anything than for their son to receive his sight—to be able to make eye contact with him and share thoughts on things of beauty.

After responding to questions from His disciples about the

Free to Shine

man born blind, Jesus spat on the ground and made clay with His saliva, then anointed the man's eyes and told him to "*Go wash in the pool of Siloam*." The man went and washed and came back seeing (John 9:1-7).

Overwhelmed with excitement, his first priority would certainly have been to see his parents' faces and rejoice with them over his newly-acquired sight. What unspeakable joy and gratitude must have flooded their souls?

After collecting themselves, surely the first question these parents would have asked is: "How did this happen?" They would have glued themselves to every detail as he recounted his awesome story.

A short time later, the man's neighbors and those who knew that he was born blind brought him before the Pharisees who inquired as to how he had acquired his sight. Refusing to believe his answer, they called for his parents whose response was quite remarkable: "*We do not know.*"

The miracle of their son's sight was the most wonderful, astonishing experience of their lives. Yet, when questioned by the Pharisees (while still in awe of the miracle), they let the fear of being ejected from the synagogue *distract* them, forfeiting their opportunity to shine by failing to witness to the truth.

Free From Distraction (from within)

> *"And they asked them, saying, 'Is this your son, who you say was born blind? How then does he now see?' His parents answered them and said, 'we know that this is our son, and that he was born blind; but by what means he now sees we do not know, or who opened his eyes we do not know. He is of age; ask him. He will speak for himself.' His parents said these things because they feared the Jews, for the Jews had agreed already that if anyone confessed that He was the Christ, he would be put out of the synagogue."*
>
> *(John 9:19-21)*

It was not for fear of safety that these parents concealed the truth, but a desire to maintain their standing within the community. Even the joy of receiving the greatest blessing imaginable may not be enough for some people to deny themselves and allow God's glory to shine as the greater priority.

> *Distractions from within are, for the most part, avoidable*

At a recent leadership meeting, I had a brief conversation

with a pastor who had been praying silently with his hands slightly raised. When I asked about his thoughts on praying in tongues, he replied: "It's a gift that God chooses to give to certain people in the Church; he has not given it to me."

"I believe it is available to everybody," I said. "God does not regard one person above another" (Acts 10:34). "Well," he fired back, "how do you explain Paul's question, *"Do all speak with tongues?"* (I Corinthians 12:30). My response brought our conversation to an abrupt end: "Is Paul referring to the *unwillingness* of the Giver (the Holy Spirit) to give this gift or to the *'unreadiness'* of the seeker to open it?"

The fact that it is commonly understood that not all Believers will speak in tongues proves that Paul's above question is rhetorical. You cannot build doctrine on a lone rhetorical question. Certainly Paul was aware that there are numerous reasons why a person may not speak in tongues. Almost anything, good or bad, can distract us away from the truth.

Distraction has become a popular tool that yields both winners and losers. Spiritual gifts help to make our senses keen to distractions. Perhaps, this is one of the reasons Paul urges his readers to earnestly desire the best spiritual gifts (I Corinthians 12:31). Distractions pave the way for powerlessness but our Lord delights to set us free.

Free From Distraction   (from within)

Our Lord delights to set us free.

Spiritual, physical, and social powerlessness is the devil's hope for all Christians

Free from Powerlessness

10

Saul, later known as Paul, is first introduced in Acts chapter seven with the story of Stephen.

"... And they cast him out of the city and stoned him. And the witnesses laid down their clothes at the feet of a young man named Saul. And they stoned Stephen as he was calling on God and saying, 'Lord Jesus, receive my spirit.'"

(Acts 7:58-59)

"As for Saul, he made havoc of the church, entering every house and dragging off men and women, committing

them to prison."

(Acts 8:3)

Saul was driven by an intensely hostile attitude towards Christians. Having letters of authority given to him by the chief priests to arrest anyone who worships the Lord Jesus Christ (Acts 9:1-2), he traumatized Christians throughout Jerusalem, leaving many families in a state of powerlessness. God only knows how many people he hurt while thinking he was right.

Powerlessness is a most unsettling feeling. Every effort should be made to avoid it, but whenever it happens (and it happens to all of us), we should learn from it while trusting God to show us the way of escape (I Corinthians 10:13).

The movie, *The Perfect Storm*, created a lasting memory for me. The fishing boat captain was confident that he and his crew would prevail against the sea, until the moment that he gazed at that insurmountable wave and said, *"She's not going to let us out."*

> *Our most vivid memories often derive from experiences with powerlessness*

After watching me swim in the deep end of the city's public

swimming pool, my best friend, who was also 10 years old, falsely assumed that he could do the same. From the moment he jumped into the water he was in trouble. The terror on his face compelled me to go after him. Upon reaching him, he grabbed me and pulled me down under him, using my body as a life raft to keep his head above water.

Struggling unsuccessfully to free myself, I experienced a level of powerlessness unlike anything before or after. In the same moment that the water claimed my last breath, my soul called out to God and the lifeguard snatched him off of me. That experience shaped a whole new attitude in me about God, powerlessness, and the preciousness of life.

Scripture makes clear God's concern for the weak and powerless: "*He gives power to the weak and to those who have no might He increases strength*" (Isaiah 40:29).

> *Few things reveal moral character like how one treats the powerless*

Therefore, before God entrusted Paul with the gospel, He had to fit him with a right attitude toward powerlessness.

11) "And I punished them often in every synagogue and

compelled them to blaspheme; and being exceedingly enraged against them, I persecuted them even to foreign cities. 12) While thus occupied, as I journeyed to Damascus with authority and commission from the chief priests, 13) at midday, O king, along the road I saw a light from heaven, brighter than the sun, shining around me and those who journeyed with me. 14) And when we all had fallen to the ground, I heard a voice speaking to me and saying in Hebrew language, 'Saul, Saul, why are you persecuting Me?'" 15) "...So I said, 'Who are You, Lord?' And He said; 'I am Jesus, whom you are persecuting.'"

(Acts 26:11-15)

The light that Paul saw along the road was the glory of the Lamb of God, the same light that will illuminate the Holy City, New Jerusalem. This encounter with Jesus was without question the most traumatizing experience of this "traumatizer's" life. Nothing (not being shipwrecked on the sea at night, stoned, beaten with rods, or even left for dead) compares with the dread of being confronted by the presence of a just, holy, and all-knowing God, while guilty of sin.

Blinded by the light, stunned by the voice, and now being

led away in the hands of a stranger, Paul's attitude towards powerlessness was being transformed. He was forced to face the trauma of being incapable of altering a distressing situation.

Perhaps Paul's blindness was also God's way of freeing him to ponder both the weightiness of his past deeds of unknowingly *persecuting God* (Acts 9:4-5) and the new life he was now being called to embrace (Acts 9:15-16). It may also have served as a positive distraction to keep him from being overburdened with grief, after realizing his responsibility in ruining the lives of God's precious followers.

One can hardly imagine the things that likely ran through Paul's mind during his three days of darkness (Galatians 1:13). His eyes reopened to a transformed reality (Acts 9:9); for with new life comes new attitude.

> *Attitude shapes our decisions and reveals the strength of our witness*

"Attitude" speaks of a manner of acting, feeling, or thinking that shows one's disposition, opinion, etc.[4] It is the disposition, feelings, actions, and moods we display in response to life happening around us.

As leaders of God's flock, it is important that we model the attitudes we teach about.

Paul understood that in order to properly imitate Jesus he would have to know Him well. So he prayed, *"That I may know Him and the power of His resurrection, and the fellowship of His suffering, being conformed to His death..."* (Philippians 3:10).

The best way to prove that you truly know Christ is to let Him be seen working in you — displaying His strength through your weakness.

> *7) "And lest I should be exalted above measure by the abundance of the revelations, a thorn in the flesh was given to me, a messenger of Satan to buffet me, lest I be exalted above measure. 8) Concerning this thing I pleaded with the Lord three times that it might depart from me. 9) And He said to me, 'My grace is sufficient for you, for My strength is made perfect in weakness.' Therefore most gladly I will rather boast in my infirmities, that the power of Christ may rest upon me. 10) Therefore I take pleasure in infirmities, in reproaches, in needs, in persecutions, in distresses, for Christ's sake. For when I am weak, then I am strong."*
>
> *(2 Corinthians 12:7-10)*

Free From Powerlessness

This is why praying in tongues is so important, for this grace-gift restores confidence that your labor is not in vain in the Lord and inspires you to be *"steadfast, immovable, always abounding in the work of the Lord"* (I Corinthians 15:58).

Armed with a new attitude towards powerlessness, Paul boldly trumpets the cause of those who are weak, vulnerable, and easily hindered or made to stumble. He devotes nearly the entire 14th chapter of Romans to this issue of moving thoughtfully among the weak with a right attitude, and he revisits it again in 1 Corinthians 8:9-13.

"It is good neither to eat meat nor drink wine nor do anything by which your brother stumbles or is offended or is made weak"

(Romans 14:21)

"But beware lest somehow this liberty of yours become a stumbling block to those who are weak."
(I Corinthians 8:9)

When we allow Christ to work in and through us, being careful not to think of ourselves more highly than we ought (Romans 12:3), we are then free to consider the helplessness of others

(Romans 12:10-21). This freedom is rooted in our obedience to God and is made clearer as we learn of the things freely given to us by God (I Corinthians 2:12).

Spiritual, physical, and social powerlessness is the devil's hope for all Christians. His aim is to put distance between God and His followers by entangling us in sin, or deceiving us to forfeit the spiritual activity that intimacy with God and love for His people would produce.

> *"Having then gifts differing according to the grace that is given to us, let us use them: if prophecy, let us prophesy in proportion to our faith; or ministry, let us use it in our ministering; he who teaches, in teaching; he who exhorts, in exhortation; he who gives, with liberality; he who leads, with diligence; he who shows mercy, with cheerfulness..."*
>
> *(Romans 12:6-8)*

Only through obedience to God's Word are we free to flee from worldly thoughts and pursuits. Opening the gift of tongues helps in forcing the devil to flee from us. Conscious knowledge of our intimate relationship with the Lord and His nearness to us is what frees us to shine....

Freedom has a certain appearance;
truth has a certain tone

Robert E. Colwell

It would strain us to fathom all the issues that go unaddressed in one year by Christians around the world who pray only in languages they understand

Conclusion

Surely, one would expect that a book dealing exclusively with opening the gift of tongues would include instructions on how to open it. The Bible offers no clear directives, however, certain passages of Scripture are insightful.

26) "Now an angel of the Lord spoke to Philip, saying, 'Arise and go toward the south along the road which goes down from Jerusalem to Gaza.' This is desert. 27) So he arose and went. And behold, a man of Ethiopia, a eunuch of great authority under Candace the Queen of the Ethiopians, who had charge of all her treasury, and had come to Jerusalem to worship, 28) was return-

ing. And sitting in his chariot, he was reading Isaiah the prophet. 29) Then the Spirit said to Philip, 'Go near and overtake this chariot.' 30) So Philip ran to him, and heard him reading the prophet Isaiah, and said, 'Do you understand what you are reading?' 31) And he said, 'How can I, unless someone guides me?' And he asked Philip to come up and sit with him. 32) The place in the Scripture which he read was this: 'He was led as a sheep to the slaughter; And as a lamb before its shearer is silent, So He opened not His mouth. 33) In His humiliation His justice was taken away, And who will declare His generation? For His life is taken from the earth.'

34) So the eunuch answered Philip and said, 'I ask you, of whom does the prophet say this, of himself or of some other man?' 35) Then Philip opened his mouth, and beginning at this Scripture, preached Jesus to him. 36) Now as they went down the road, they came to some water. And the eunuch said, 'See, here is water. What hinders me from being baptized?' 37) Then Philip said, 'if you believe with all your heart, you may.' And he answered and said, 'I believe that Jesus Christ is the Son of God.' 38) So he commanded the chariot to stand still. And both Philip and the eunuch went down into the water, and

Conclusion

he baptized him. 39) Now when they came up out of the water, the Spirit of the Lord caught Philip away, so that the eunuch saw him no more; and he went on his way rejoicing."

(Acts 8:26-39)

The steps leading to baptism in the Spirit (preparing the Christian to open the gift of tongues) are much the same as for water baptism. One difference is that with water baptism, another person pronounces your relationship with the Lord; with praying in tongues, you yourself must pronounce that you have received and opened this gift.

Four steps to opening the gift of tongues that parallel water baptism:
- Be acquainted with what Scripture says about it (Acts 8:30-35)
- Come with an attitude of worship (Acts 8:27-28), (Psalms 19:14)
- Make sure you are free of hindrances, then ask (Acts 8:36)
- Believe with all your heart that praying in tongues will enhance your spiritual life, and then open your mouth in faith and speak (Acts 8:37)

Keep in mind: the above is *suggestive*, only. Your experience may be different. For some, it may happen immediately—with or without asking for it (although, nothing happens without prayer). Others may experience a time of cleansing and growing while they wait (usually not long if the above steps have been implemented).

Because the gift of tongues is often referred to as being baptized in the Spirit, many who have not had this experience take offence at the suggestion that they lack the Holy Spirit's infilling power. Truth is, all who accept Jesus Christ as Lord and Savior have received the Holy Spirit and are part of the Body of Christ.

But not all are ready (whether unaware or unwilling) to avail themselves to the life-altering, ministry-empowering transformation that accompanies a full release of the Holy Spirit into one's personal being.

This has long been a divisive issue for the Church. Therefore, my approach to this subject is with the presumption that those who read this book are at least casually interested in opening the gift of tongues (if they have not done so already), or they desire a better understanding and ability to explain it to others.

If a person is unaware that they have money in their pocket, they will bypass opportunities to buy. Likewise, if you do not know that you have the capacity to speak in tongues, no effort

Conclusion

will be made to do so.

Praying in tongues is an added benefit of God's grace that allows us to express the depths of our soul with a greater sense of connectedness and urgency. It is a faith-building inner witness that highlights our personal relationship with God. It is not a replacement for general prayer, for such is the Christian's way of life.

The difference in these two kinds of prayers came to light for me some years ago when seeing a frightful-looking man pushing a cart by the roadside. So disturbingly grave was his appearance that without the gift of tongues, I would have been at a loss for how to pray for him. He looked like he existed on a diet of dangerous drugs and appeared to be suffering from multiple diseases.

When I opened my mouth to pray, the thoughts of my heart gushed out in a powerful language, which could only come by way of grace. And although it took days to clear my head of that hideous image, I took comfort knowing that my prayer for the man had been accurately and thoroughly conveyed.

Prayer changes things

Free to Shine

Ever consider the number of issues that you daily neglect to pray for because you lacked time, energy, or the right words to say? Multiply that number by the number of days in a year, then by the number of people in your church that do not pray in tongues, and you can begin to understand the value of this spiritual gift.

It would strain us to fathom all the issues that go unaddressed in one year by Christians around the world who pray only in languages they understand. No wonder the devil discourages the use of this gift. He is fully aware of the power and benefits of praying in tongues, which is kind-of-like talking to God in a secured space, free of menacing distractions—including having to figure out the right words to say.

Of the many who do pray in tongues, there are those who have only a shallow understanding of the purpose and power of this gift. Not only does it afford a Believer the confidence to shine, it is also perhaps the best tool for reversing the present ruinous reorienting of our young people. It helps them to keep their eyes focused on the prize, which is Christ.

My aim in writing this book is to hopefully *'run up alongside someone's chariot,'* as Philip did for the eunuch (Acts 8:29), and provide:

- knowledge of the purpose and power of praying in tongues

Conclusion

- guidance for those longing to know the Lord on a deeper level
- inspiration to experience all the grace that the Holy Spirit delights to give

My hope is that all who long to open this gift will ask of themselves the same question that the eunuch asked Philip: *"What hinders me from being baptized?"*

The eunuch needed Philip's assistance for water baptism (Acts 8:29-36). You, however, need only the knowledge and confidence that this gift can be opened today in order to *speak in tongues*.

Find a comfortable space to pray, cleanse your mind of distractions, open your heart to the Lord in worship, and then open your mouth in praise to God—expecting the Holy Spirit to assist you.

> *"For the promise is to you and to your children, and to all who are afar off, as many as the Lord our God will call" (Acts 2:39)*

Even before fully understanding the Scriptures regarding tongues, I sensed that God would not deny anyone who earnestly desired to have this experience. Grace does not discriminate.

Its appeal is always to "Whoever."

Matthew 12:50 – *"For whoever does the will of my Father in heaven is My brother and sister and mother."*

Matthew 13:12 – *"To whoever has, to him much more will be given."*

John 3:15 – *"...That whoever believes in Him should not perish but have eternal life."*

Romans 10:11-13 – *"For the Scripture says, 'Whoever believes on Him will not be put to shame.' For there is no distinction between Jew and Greek, for the same Lord over all is rich to all who call upon Him. For 'whoever calls on the name of the Lord shall be saved.'"*

> *"Jesus Christ is the same yesterday, today, and forever"* (Hebrews 13:8)

It would be totally out of character for God to single out certain Believers to experience His divine gift and, without explanation, deny others. As a result of wrong teaching, some desiring to have this experience have dabbled in the ridiculous trying to produce something of the same.

Conclusion

"You shall know the truth and the truth shall make you free."

(John 8:32)

I believe the Bible is the inspired breathed-out Word of God, and that all of its grace gifts are available to be used today. There will always be those who will challenge the applicability of Scriptures related to this issue and will label those who promote this experience as deceived or confused.

No wonder Paul waited a number of years before sharing with the Corinthians about having heard words not lawful for a man to utter (II Corinthians 12:3-5).

Since none of us have heard such words, an abundance of caution should precede any decision to discount or dismiss Paul's teachings. Praying in tongues serves to build us up, empowering us to deal effectively with our issues. A collective sense of urgency in teaching about this gift will go a long way in freeing Believers to shine in these difficult days.

Current threats against the Christian way of life should bring to mind God's Word to Israel: *"No weapon formed against you shall prosper, and every tongue which rises against you in judgment you shall condemn"* (Isaiah 54:17). Our prayer should be that Christians throughout the world would encourage others as

Paul did Timothy: *"Stir up this gift of God which is in you through the laying on of my hands"* (II Timothy 1:6).

Christians who have slacked off from praying in tongues should identify and eliminate the distractions that have hindered them. The devil's deceptions are strong. Young people today are particularly vulnerable.

Those who understand and treasure opening this grace gift have a responsibility to share their faith and their experiences with others; for in the days ahead, many will need to open this gift. It will prove to be a powerful tool for standing and navigating a path through this present darkness.

> *"For the promise is to you and to your children, and to all who are afar off, as many as the Lord our God will call"*
> *(Acts 2:39)*

Sources

1 Webster's New World College Dictionary, Fourth Edition. 1999

2 Ibid., p. 46

3 Danker, Frederick William. A Greek-English Lexicon of the New Testament and Other Early. Christian Literature. Chicago: The University of Chicago Press, 2000.

4 Ibid., p. 57

About the Author

Robert E. Colwell is the senior pastor of Calvary Chapel Crenshaw in Los Angeles and a lifelong advocate for displaced children. He has been the keynote speaker and trainer at state and national foster care conferences in 27 states and has hosted marriage conferences and workshops for over 28 years. His journey through foster care is woven into powerful insights in his book, *Love Leaves No Regrets*. Robert earned a Master's degree in theology from Fuller Theological Seminary in 2004. He and his wife, Angela, live in Inglewood, California and have four adult children.

Notes

Notes

Notes

www.ingramcontent.com/pod-product-compliance
Lightning Source LLC
LaVergne TN
LVHW041301080426
835510LV00009B/824